W9-CBJ-076

In memory of my sister, Pam

Text copyright © 2009 by Robbin Gourley

All rights reserved. Originally published in hardcover in the United States by Clarion Books,
an imprint of Houghton Mifflin Harcourt Publishing Company, 2009.

Recipes on page 45 from *Sugar Pie & Jelly Roll* by Robbin Gourley, © 2000 by Robbin Gourley.
Reprinted by permission of Algonquin Books of Chapel Hill.

For information about permission to reproduce selections from this book,
write to trade.permissions@hmhco.com or to Permissions,
Houghton Mifflin Harcourt Publishing Company, 3 Park Avenue, 19th Floor, New York, New York 10016.

www.hmhco.com

Hand-lettering by John Stevens.
The illustrations were executed in watercolor.
The text was set in 15-point Old Claude LP.

The Library of Congress has cataloged the hardcover edition as follows:
Gourley, Robbin.
Bring me some apples and I'll make you a pie: a story about Edna Lewis/by Robbin Gourley.
p. cm.
Summary: From the whippoorwill's call on the first day of spring through the first snowfall,
Edna and members of her family gather fruits, berries, and vegetables from the fields, garden, and orchard on their
Virginia farm and turn them into wonderful meals. Includes facts about the life of Edna Lewis,
a descendant of slaves who grew up to be a famous chef, and five recipes.
1. Lewis, Edna—Childhood and youth—Juvenile fiction. [1. Lewis, Edna—childhood and youth—Fiction.
2. Harvesting—Fiction. 3. Farm life—Fiction. 4. Family life—Virginia—Fiction. 5. Cookery—Fiction.
6. African Americans—Fiction. 7. Virginia—History—1865–1950—Fiction.] Title.
PZ7.G7387Bri2009
[E]—dc22 2007046978

ISBN: 978-0-618-15836-2 hardcover
ISBN: 978-0-544-80901-7 paperback

Manufactured in China
SCP 10 9 8 7 6 5 4 3 2 1
4500595895

Bring Me Some Apples and I'll Make You a Pie

A Story About Edna Lewis

by Robbin Gourley

Houghton Mifflin Harcourt
Boston   New York

Whippoorwill! calls the little gray bird. *Whippoorwill! Whippoorwill!* The melody echoes through the quiet woods and wends its way down the hill to the just-waking farm.

This is the sound Edna's been waiting for all winter long. "Time to get up!" she says, poking her sleepy little sister. "I hear the whippoorwill. That means it's gathering time. I'm ready for the taste of spring."

oorWiLL !

After breakfast, Edna and her sister head out to the fields to pick wild strawberries, the first fruit of the season.

Mama says, "Better hurry! You'll need to outrun the rabbits to get all the berries."

Daddy says, "Fill as many baskets as you can. Larder's empty."

Sister says, "One for the basket and one to taste."
Edna says, "There'll be strawberry shortcake for dessert tonight!"

A few days later, with the chill almost gone from the early morning air, Auntie and the children gather wild greens before the leaves unfurl: mustard, purslane, dandelion, and peppery watercress, too.

"*Mmm-mmm!*" says Auntie. "A fresh, crisp salad to nourish the heart and soul as well as the body."

Edna recites:

"*But I have never tasted meat,*
nor cabbage, corn, or beans,
nor milk or tea that's half as sweet
as that first mess of greens."

Soon the catbird is back and the dogwoods are blooming. Edna follows Daddy behind the plow, pressing her bare feet into the soft, just-turned earth. The plow tosses up roots from the nearby sassafras trees, each piece a prize in Edna's hands.

Edna says, "I'll make hot tea from the roots and sweeten it with milk and molasses."

Daddy says:
"Sassafras heals what ails you.
Sassafras makes you feel all right.
Drink the tea in the morning
and sleep all night."

Spring turns into summer, and
Edna leads Daddy to a beehive she's found
deep in the fragrant honeysuckle woods. He breaks the
comb and gathers all the delicious dark-amber nectar.

Edna dips her finger in the bucket. "Honey on hot
biscuits sweetens the morning," she says, smacking her lips.
Then she recites:

> *A swarm of bees in May is worth a load of hay.*
> *A swarm of bees in June is worth a silver spoon.*
> *A swarm of bees in July is not worth a fly.*"

14

A warm breeze is blowing, and it's cherry-picking time. Everyone races to the trees and up the ladders to fill buckets and bellies with the ripe fruit.

Edna says, "A deep-dish cherry pie—that'll be the reward for all our hard work."

Brother says:

"*Look at that bird in the cherry tree.*
He's eating them one by one.
He's shaking his bill, he's getting his fill
as down his throat they run."

When the wild blackberries are ripe, Edna, Sister, and Brother forage early in the day, before thunderstorms start to rumble. Sweet berries stain hands and lips and teeth blue.

Brother says, "The ripe ones come easiest off the vine, and the lowest ones are the sweetest. Watch out for snakes! They like berries, too."

Edna calls across the brambles, "How about we make a summer pudding or a cobbler? Or just have a bowlful of berries with sugar and cream?"

Oh, the blackberry!

Summer Pudding?

Blackberry Cobbler?

Long about midsummer, it's time to gather sun-ripened peaches from the orchard. Edna eats them straight from the tree, and the warm, sweet juice runs down her chin.

Mama says, "Six perfect peaches make a perfect pie."

"That's true," Edna says. "But the best dessert on a hot summer day is peach ice cream, and there'll be plenty of willing hands to help turn the crank on the ice cream bucket."

"Peaches!" Auntie sighs. "Pure as angels. Sweet as love."

Edna plucks garden-warmed tomatoes from a vine heavy with fruit and places them in Mama's outstretched apron.

"Southern dirt mixed with southern sun makes a right sassy tomato," Mama says. "My favorite lunch above all is a tangy tomato sandwich."

Sugar baby watermelons ripen in the fields. As the sun sets, the family gathers round, and Daddy plugs the melons till he finds a perfect one.

"Melons are just like friends," Granny says. "Gotta try ten before you get a good one."

Everyone savors the crisp, cool, juicy slices. The children spit the seeds as far as they can.

Daddy says, "Save some of those seeds to plant for new melons."

Between slurps, Edna says, "Save the rinds! We'll make watermelon pickle."

In high summer, even mornings are hot and dry. Edna, Brother, and Sister stand at the edge of the cornfield, in the shade of the pine trees where the night's coolness still hovers.

"Corn on the cob makes the best summer supper," says Brother.

"I say it's corn pudding that does that," says Edna.

"Skillet cornbread is *my* favorite," says Sister. Then she sings:
    "Wake up, Jacon. Day's a-breakin'.
    Fryin' pan's on and cornbread's bakin'.
    Bacon in the pan. Coffee in the pot.
    Git up now and get it while it's hot."

Out in the vegetable patch, tidy rows of beans are ready for the picking. Bushel baskets fill quickly as three pairs of hands make a game of pulling beans from the bushes.

"A bowl of speckled butter beans for dinner tonight!" says Sister.

"Rattlesnake and Christmas beans next," says Edna.

"We're rich as kings as long as we have beans," says Mama.

Edna skips beside Brother down the farm lane to the leafy vineyard. Sunny clusters of muscadine grapes grow in wild abundance, vines twined to the treetops. Ripe grapes make a perfect afternoon feast.

"I love the jam these grapes will make," Edna says. "Come winter, it'll be a little taste of summer."

Brother nods. "On a cold day, there's nothing more comforting than a thick slice of bread piled high with Mama's grape jam."

It's back to school just as the apples start to ripen. They crunch with every bite and taste as sweet as honeycomb.

"There's so much to do with good apples!" says Edna. "With bushels of apples in the cellar, we'll have apple butter and apple cider and applesauce all winter long. But today I'll make apple crisp, sweet and tart at the same time."

Then she sings:

> "Don't ask me no questions,
>   an' I won't tell you no lies.
>   But bring me some apples,
>   an' I'll make you some pies.
>   And if you ask questions
>   'bout my havin' the flour,
>   I'll forget to use 'lasses,
>   an' the pie'll be sour."

Ping

Ping

On a coming-of-winter morning,
there's still one more harvest to gather.
The leaves are falling, and so are the nuts.
Ping-ping-ping. Pecans and walnuts
clatter on the rooftop. The family fills
baskets full of them.

Edna cracks the shells and picks
out the tiny nutmeats. "Nut-butter
cookies and walnut bread will taste
mighty good," she says.

Then Granny sings:

> *"Raccoon up the pecan tree.*
> *Possum on the ground.*
> *Raccoon shake the pecans down.*
> *Possum pass 'em round."*

35

As the first snow falls, Edna inspects the cellar. It is full of good things: nut cakes and cookies, honey and jam, three kinds of dried beans. Rows of canned corn, jars of tomatoes, and crocks of pickles line the shelves.

"You can never have too much summer," says Edna.

The house fills with the aromas of cooking, warming the spirit on a cold afternoon.

"Long winter ahead," says Daddy.

"Without winter, there'd be no spring," says Mama.

"That's right," says Edna. "And come spring, we'll hear the whippoorwill call. Then we'll all go gathering again!"

AUTHOR'S NOTE

Edna Lewis was born in 1916, in Freetown, Virginia, a community founded by her grandfather and two other emancipated slaves. The people of Freetown were farmers, and they lived by the seasons, growing and harvesting their own crops, gathering nature's wild bounty.

Edna learned to cook by helping her mother and her aunt Jenny prepare meals for their extended family. She was taught that fruits and vegetables taste best when they're sun-ripened and freshly picked. She learned that loving the land and tending gardens produces happy, healthy, long-lived people and thriving communities.

When she grew up, Edna became a famous chef and worked in restaurants in both northern and southern cities. Her approach to cooking won her many awards and honors, and she wrote four cookbooks to teach people how to prepare food in the Southern regional style. But her most significant contribution was to make people aware of the importance of preserving traditional methods of growing and preparing food and of bringing ingredients directly from the field to the table. Edna retired as a chef in 1992 and died at the age of 89 at her home in Decatur, Georgia.

In creating this book, I was strongly influenced by glorious childhood summers spent on my grandmother's farm in North Carolina, growing, gathering, preparing, and eating delicious food from the garden. During that time, I was dosed with plenty of fanciful and humorous garden lore by the grownups working the farm. Some of these rhymes and sayings are in the book; others I've included were taken from American folk tradition.

From this experience and from my research, I could easily imagine what Edna's childhood might have been like. As a student of Southern cooking and as a food writer, I have also been inspired by Edna's cookbooks and

JAMES MARSHALL/CORBIS

CHEF EDNA LEWIS IN THE DINING ROOM OF
GAGE & TOLLNER, BROOKLYN, N.Y., 1989

by her philosophy. For Edna, the goal was to coax the best flavor from each
ingredient, and the reward was the taste and satisfaction of a delicious meal.

On the next few pages, you'll find recipes—updated for the modern
cook—that represent the kind of dishes Edna Lewis loved. They're meant
to be made with adult supervision and enjoyed by the whole family. You
can find Edna's own recipes in the following cookbooks.

The Edna Lewis Cookbook (Ecco, 1989)
In Pursuit of Flavor by Edna Lewis (University of Virginia Press, 2000)
*The Gift of Southern Cooking: Recipes and Revelations from Two Great American
Cooks* by Edna Lewis and Scott Peacock (Knopf, 2003)
The Taste of Country Cooking by Edna Lewis (Knopf, 2007)

STRAWBERRY SHORTCAKE

Serves 8

Filling
6 cups fresh strawberries plus
    1 cup for garnish
⅓ cup sugar

Whipped cream
½ pint heavy cream
    (or whipping cream), chilled
Sugar to taste

Shortcake
¼ cup sugar plus ½ tablespoon sugar
2½ cups unbleached, all-purpose flour
    plus 2 tablespoons for dusting
½ cup (1 stick) cold butter, cut into pieces,
    plus 2 tablespoons, melted
2½ teaspoons baking powder
1 teaspoon salt
1 cup whole milk

Rinse and hull the strawberries. If they are large, cut them in halves or quarters. Sprinkle with ⅓ cup sugar. Let stand at room temperature until syrupy, turning occasionally, about 1 hour.

Place the heavy cream in a metal bowl and chill in the refrigerator until ready to whip.

Preheat the oven to 425 degrees. Lightly grease a baking sheet with butter.

In a food processor, combine ¼ cup sugar, 2½ cups flour, cut-up butter, baking powder, and salt. Process lightly until the mixture resembles coarse meal but lumps the size of small peas remain. Add milk and pulse processor 4 or 5 times, until dough is just mixed. Do not over-process. The dough should be moist and sticky. (You can also use two knives, a pastry blender, or your fingers to mix the ingredients together.)

Sprinkle 2 tablespoons of flour on a countertop or large cutting board. Spread the flour in a circle. Remove the blade from the food processor and scrape off the dough onto the floured countertop. With floured fingers, scoop the dough out of the food processor onto the floured surface. Gently pat dough into a 4″ x 8″ rectangle. For a light, fluffy shortcake, handle the dough as little as possible.

Dust a large knife with flour and cut the dough into 8 squares. Transfer them to the greased baking sheet. Brush them with melted butter and sprinkle with ½ tablespoon sugar.

Place the baking sheet on the middle rack of the oven and bake squares until golden, 20–25 minutes. Allow to cool on baking sheet.

Whip the chilled heavy cream with an electric beater or in a mixer. Add sugar to desired sweetness.

To serve, split the shortcakes with a serrated knife. Spoon a generous helping of the sweetened berries over the bottom of each shortcake. Cover with the top half and top with a generous dollop of whipped cream. Garnish with a spoonful of berries.

CORN PUDDING

Serves 6 to 8

3 tablespoons unsalted butter, melted,
    plus more for greasing the casserole dish
4 fresh, uncooked ears of corn
¼ cup sugar
1 teaspoon salt

2 large eggs
2 cups whole milk
Pinch of cayenne pepper
½ teaspoon freshly grated nutmeg
2 tablespoons cornmeal

Preheat the oven to 350 degrees. Butter a 1½-quart casserole dish.

Remove the husks and silk from the corn. Rinse under cold water and drain. Holding the ear vertically and slicing from the top to the bottom, cut the kernels from each cob onto a cutting board. There should be about two cups of kernels. Scrape the corn from the cutting board into a large bowl. Add the sugar and salt and stir well.

In a separate, smaller bowl, whisk the eggs. Add milk, pouring in a steady stream while whisking. Add melted butter, cayenne pepper, and nutmeg and stir. Pour the mixture into the corn-and-sugar mixture.

Dust the buttered casserole dish with cornmeal. Pour the mixture into the dish and place the dish in a deep, sturdy roasting pan. Then fill the pan with boiling water until it reaches halfway up the sides of the casserole dish. (This is called a *bain-marie*.)

Place the pan on the middle rack of the oven and bake for 1 hour or until the pudding is gently set and the top lightly browned.

Serve immediately or let set for up to 30 minutes before serving.

APPLE CRISP

Serves 6 to 8

Apples
6 cups peeled, cored, sliced
    apples, about 2 to 3 pounds
¼ teaspoon cinnamon, or
    more to taste
2 tablespoons sugar
¼ cup orange juice

Topping
¼ teaspoon cinnamon
½ cup sugar
5 tablespoons butter plus more for
    greasing the pan
¾ cup rolled oats
½ cup walnuts or pecans

Preheat oven to 375 degrees. Lightly butter an 8-inch square or 9-inch round baking pan.

Mix together ¼ teaspoon cinnamon and 2 tablespoons sugar. Toss the apple slices with the orange juice to coat, sprinkle on the cinnamon sugar, and mix well. Then spread the apples in the buttered pan.

Place topping ingredients in a food processor and pulse a few times, until ingredients are just combined. Do not puree. (You can also mix ingredients by hand. Just soften butter slightly, toss together dry ingredients, and work butter in with fingertips, a pastry blender, or a fork.)

Spread topping over apples and bake about 40 minutes, until topping is browned and apples are tender. Serve hot, warm, or at room temperature.

Note: For best results, use tart apples, such as Macintosh or Stayman Winesap (Edna's favorite), for this recipe.

PECAN DROPS

2½ to 3 dozen cookies

½ cup butter plus more for greasing
   the cookie sheet
1 cup light brown sugar
1 egg, well beaten
½ cup unbleached, all-purpose flour

¼ teaspoon salt
1 teaspoon vanilla
1 cup chopped pecans

Preheat oven to 350 degrees. Grease cookie sheet.

In a medium bowl, use a mixer to cream butter and sugar until light and fluffy. Add egg, flour, and salt and mix well. Add vanilla and pecans and blend.

Drop by the teaspoonful onto greased cookie sheet and bake on the middle rack of the oven for 10 minutes or until lightly browned. Remove while still warm. Cool on racks. Store in an airtight container.

NUT-BUTTER SQUARES

36 squares

1 cup sugar
1 cup butter
2 cups unbleached, all-purpose flour

2 tablespoons vanilla
1 egg, separated
2 cups chopped walnuts

Preheat oven to 325 degrees.

In a medium bowl, use a mixer to cream together sugar and butter. Add flour, vanilla, and egg yolk. The dough will be stiff.

Using your hands, press dough into an 11″ x 15″ jellyroll pan. Brush dough with lightly beaten egg white. Sprinkle pecans across the dough; then press them into the dough with your fingers.

Bake on the middle rack of the oven for 25–30 minutes. (The pecans may brown quickly and burn, so check often.) Let cool for 5 minutes and cut into squares. Store in an airtight container.